This book belongs to

_____

ISBN: 979-8-9911094-0-6
Printed in the United States of America

Dear Readers, Listeners and Learners,

This book is your guide into the amazing world of SELF-LOVE! It's perfect for those first hearing about SELF-LOVE and those who want to learn more about the word. SELF-LOVE is all about YOUR well-being and happiness.

As you dive into this exciting journey, think of yourself as an adventurous explorer and be kind to yourself. Just remember, it may take some time to get the hang of it. This book is here to be your friend on your journey of discovering yourself. Discovering yourself is like finding out all the awesome things that make you, well, you! Along the way, you may also learn about other topics such as self-awareness, self-esteem, self-reflection, and self-confidence. These things might seem a bit tricky at first, but with some practice, you'll become a pro!

Remember that YOU are incredibly important. There is no one else quite like YOU, and that makes YOU super special!

-Cristina

Welcome To
LIFE-IMALS
VILLAGE

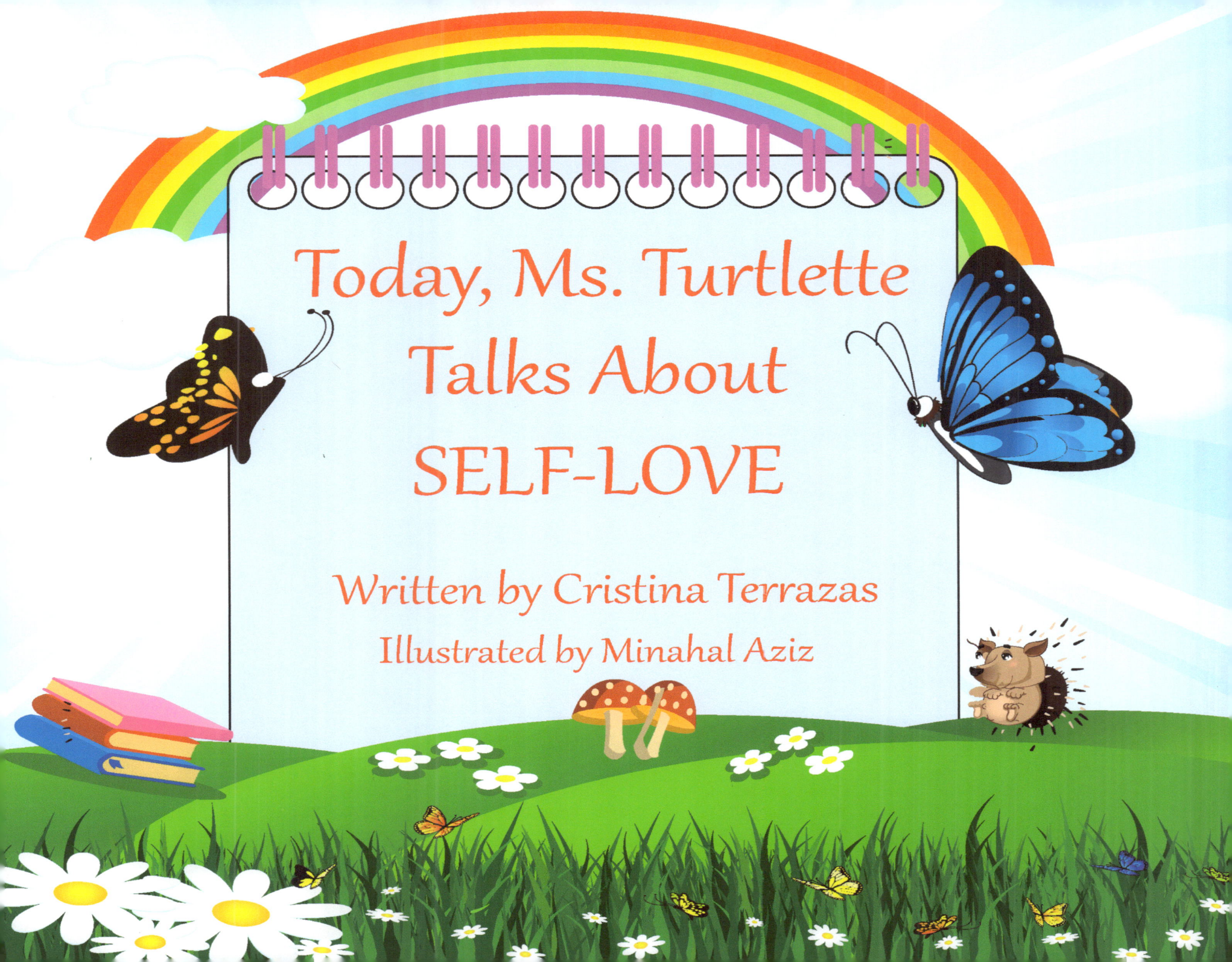

"There is something I want to **share.**
Dare I do it?"

Asks Ms. Turtlette, the teacher.

"Ok, absolutely,"
she shares gladly.

"Today, I am going to **tell you** about **SELF-LOVE,"** Ms. Turtlette says.

With wonder in her eyes,
Willow the Ooowl says,
"I've never heard that word before!
What does it mean?"

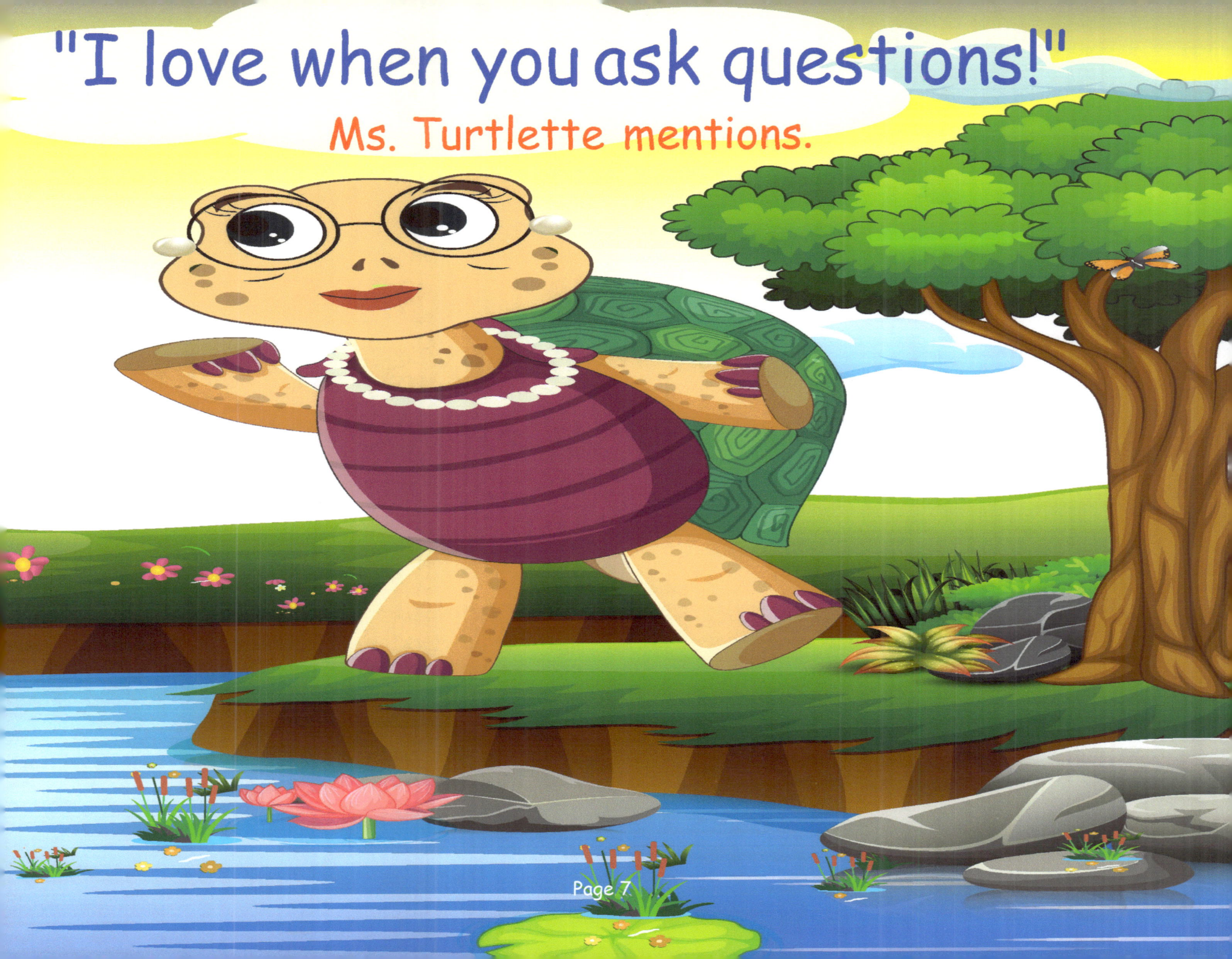

"SELF-LOVE is when YOU LOVE YOURSELF FROM THE INSIDE OUT and OUTSIDE IN," Ms. Turtlette lovingly says.

Page 8

She then tells
Willow the Ooowl and her friends,
"It's when your feelings,
thoughts, and wants
are
important."

"YOU can show **SELF-LOVE** in many **different** ways.

Ms. Turtlette sits for a bit in her favorite pond, as she shares her words, "Look at yourself in a mirror, put your hands on your heart and say to you,

I LOVE YOU!"

"Breathe in and let your love flow like a breeze.

Give yourself a hug and squeeze," Ms. Turtlette states.

"Write yourself a letter with kind words.

Dear_____,

_____

_____

_____

_____

_____

_____

_____

From_____

Mail it to you too,"

Ms. Turtlette says.

From Me

To Me

NEW YORK, NY
DEC 19
Albany, 1998

She adds, "You can do things for you too. Like brushing your teeth and washing your hair.

Create your own art. Draw, color, or paint."

"Here

and here,"
your favorite turtle teacher utters.

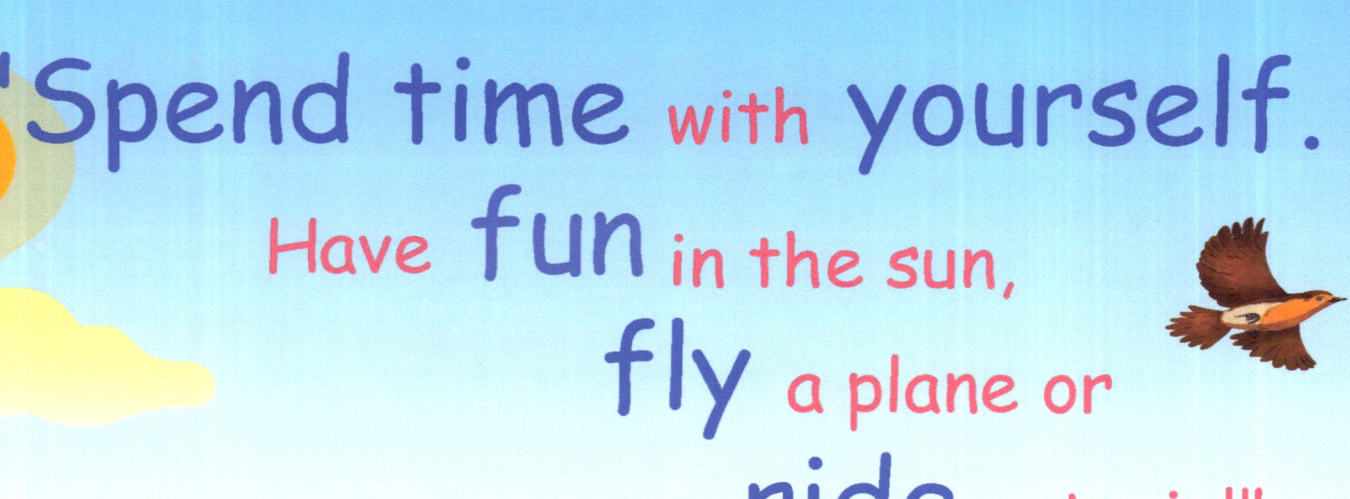

"Spend time with yourself.
Have fun in the sun,
fly a plane or
ride a train!"

After she shares her words, she sits back on her chair and closes her eyes with a smile.

She imagines having fun while sitting under the sun.

"Love yourself every day!

On **weekdays**, play days, holidays, and **even** on bad days," she adds.

Ms. Turtlette then says "Give yourself a lot or a little or somewhere in the middle.

Be sure to always ACCEPT it!"

Ms. Turtlette finishes with "Always REMEMBER

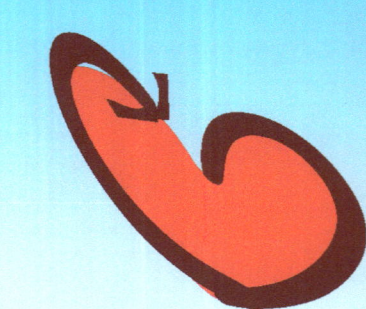

SELF LOVE NEVER ENDS!"

Come Back Soon

Glossary

Feeling- an expressive state of emotion or reaction.

Important-of great value, significance or worth.

Self-awareness- the ability to understand one's own actions, beliefs, character, emotions, motives, thoughts, and values and how they influence behavior.

Self-confidence-an attitude about one's skills and abilities.

Self-discovery- the process of understanding your true self, values, needs and wants.

Self-esteem-how one feels about themselves.

Self-love- love of self, regard of one's own well-being and happiness.

Self-reflection- meditation or serious thought about one's character, motives and actions,

Teach-explain, show.

Dedications

Dear Kieran and Zara,

Keep dreaming, dancing and playing in the mud while living in love and light.

-Nana

Thank you

Mom, Paul and Anna Terrazas, Thank you for giving me strength and direction when I needed it.

Johnny Ramirez, Thank you for your love and encouragement. I wouldn't be me without you.

Shiela Wood, Thank you for continuously suggesting I write after I told you that writing was a dream I never believed I could or would ever fulfill. This is the result of me finally believing I could, so I did.

Samantha Terrazas, Samantha Reynolds, Alexandra Swan, Elizabeth Nolasco, Frank Rubba, Diana Maldonado, Dominique Matalon, Tami Nicoll, Mary Picard, Claudine Kittle, Christine Logan, Elijah Berris Reid, Andy Roman, Susan Foti, Melissa Shoer, Gladys Perez, and Carolyn Bowsery Julia, Thank you for listening, questioning or correcting me.

To those who love to read, ENJOY!

To those who do not, focus on reading about what you like and be patient with yourself.

-Cristina

Author

Cristina Terrazas's goal is to write children's books with creative, charismatic, and curious characters while sharing marvelous stories for readers, listeners, and learners.

Some of her hobbies are sewing, photography, and writing. She lives in Palm Beach County, Florida.

Cristina had a dream to take a road trip and add color to others' self-discovery world by sharing her book, "Today, Ms. Turtlette Talks About SELF-LOVE" in EVERY STATE in the U.S.
So, Cristina decided to make her dream come true. HURRAY! Cristina, Ms. Turtlette, Willow, and her friends from LIFE-IMALS VILLAGE started their road trip in July 2024.

Illustrator

Minahal Aziz is a dedicated children's book illustrator.

She lives in Islamabad, Pakistan.

www.ingramcontent.com/pod-product-compliance
Lightning Source LLC
Chambersburg PA
CBHW040438150626

46551CB00024B/590